CIGARETTE SMUGGLING

Federal Law Enforcement Efforts and Seizures Increasing

Because of its clandestine nature, the extent of cigarette smuggling into the United States is impossible to measure with any certainty. According to ICE and ATF, investigations and intelligence collected indicate cigarette smuggling is a significant problem, particularly the smuggling of counterfeit cigarettes. According to ATF, illegal cigarette trafficking worldwide is a multibillion dollar a year crime phenomenon, with some cigarette smugglers having ties to terrorist groups. Moreover, because smuggled cigarettes are not taxed, federal and state revenues are lost. Smuggled cigarettes, which include counterfeit and genuine brand cigarettes, also pose a public health risk as all cigarettes do, but no studies have been done to determine whether counterfeit cigarettes pose any additional health risk.

ICE and ATF have been conducting more cigarette smuggling investigations in recent years. Their investigations are generally larger, more complex, and longer-term than previous investigations. Also, CBP and ICE have been seizing an increasing number of cigarettes, particularly counterfeit cigarettes, as criminals attempt to smuggle them into the United States.

Two proposed legal initiatives are intended to enhance law enforcement efforts to thwart the smuggling of cigarettes into the United States. For example, a bill known as the Prevent All Cigarette Trafficking Act would lower the threshold for a cigarette smuggling violation (a felony) from 60,000 to 10,000 cigarettes, increase ATF's authority to enter premises to enforce federal cigarette laws, and provide ATF the authority to use money generated during undercover sting operations to offset investigative expenses. In addition, the Framework Convention on Tobacco Control, a proposed international treaty, includes provisions that seek to eliminate the illicit trade in tobacco products, including cigarette smuggling.

The Departments of Homeland Security and Justice reviewed a draft of this report and had no substantive comments. Technical comments were incorporated as appropriate.

Smuggled Counterfeit Cigarettes Disguised as Legitimate Merchandise

Source: CBP.

Contents

Abbreviations

ATF	Bureau of Alcohol, Tobacco, Firearms and Explosives
ATS	Automated Targeting System
CBP	Customs and Border Protection
CCTA	Contraband Cigarette Trafficking Act
CDC	Centers for Disease Control and Prevention
DHS	Department of Homeland Security
FCTC	Framework Convention on Tobacco Control
ICE	Immigration and Customs Enforcement
IPR Center	National Intellectual Property Rights Coordination Center
IRC	Internal Revenue Code
MRU	Manifest Review Unit
PACT Act	Prevent All Cigarette Trafficking Act
TTB	Alcohol and Tobacco Tax and Trade Bureau
WHO	World Health Organization

G A O

Accountability * Integrity * Reliability

United States General Accounting Office
Washington, DC 20548

May 28, 2004

The Honorable Tom Davis
Chairman, Committee on Government Reform
House of Representatives

The Honorable Henry A. Waxman
Ranking Minority Member
Committee on Government Reform
House of Representatives

Illegal trafficking in cigarettes can generate enormous profits and is purportedly a multibillion dollar a year enterprise. As cigarette taxes increase, so do the incentives for criminal organizations, including terrorist organizations, to smuggle cigarettes into and throughout the United States. Because cigarette smuggling, whether of genuine or counterfeit cigarettes,[1] results in lost tax revenues, undermines government health policy objectives, can attract sophisticated and organized criminal groups, and could be a source of funding for terrorists, we are providing information about cigarette smuggling and efforts to combat it. More specifically, this report

- addresses the nature and scope of the problem of cigarette smuggling, including counterfeit cigarettes, into the United States and its consequences, including federal tax revenue losses and potential health risks;

- describes federal law enforcement agencies' efforts to thwart the smuggling of cigarettes into the United States; and

- identifies certain legal initiatives being pursued to enhance law enforcement efforts to thwart the smuggling of cigarettes into the United States.

To determine what is known about the nature and scope of the problem of smuggled cigarettes and law enforcement efforts to combat the problem, we obtained information from the Department of Homeland Security's

---

[1]Counterfeit cigarettes are cigarettes produced without the authorization of the trademark holder.

GAO-04-641 Cigarette Smuggling

(DHS) U.S. Immigration and Customs Enforcement (ICE) and U.S. Customs and Border Protection (CBP), and the Department of Justice's Bureau of Alcohol, Tobacco, Firearms and Explosives (ATF) officials. We also obtained information from Justice, State, and Treasury Department officials on existing legal initiatives proposed to enhance efforts to thwart cigarette smuggling. To obtain information about the health consequences of smuggled counterfeit cigarettes, we contacted the Centers for Disease Control and Prevention (CDC) and officials from the tobacco industry.

We conducted our work between August 2003 and March 2004 in accordance with generally accepted government auditing standards. (See app. I for details about our scope and methodology.)

Results in Brief

Because of its clandestine nature, the extent of cigarette smuggling into the United States is impossible to measure with any certainty. According to ICE and ATF officials, the results of investigations and intelligence collected indicate cigarette smuggling, particularly of counterfeit cigarettes, is a significant problem. Illegal cigarette trafficking worldwide is a multibillion dollar a year crime phenomenon, according to ATF, with some cigarette smugglers having ties to terrorist groups.[2] Moreover, ICE and ATF officials said that criminal organizations smuggle cigarettes into the United States, providing the organizations with the potential to garner large illegal profits. Correspondingly, because smuggled cigarettes are not taxed, federal and state revenues are lost. Smuggled cigarettes also pose a public health risk, as do all cigarettes. However, no studies have been done to determine whether counterfeit cigarettes pose any additional health risk.

ICE, ATF, and CBP carry out activities to combat the smuggling of cigarettes into the United States. ICE and ATF have been conducting more cigarette smuggling investigations in recent years. Agency officials describe their current investigations as generally larger, more complex, and longer-term than previous investigations. In addition, CBP and ICE have been seizing an increasing number of cigarettes, particularly counterfeit cigarettes, as criminals attempt to smuggle them into the United States.

---

[2]See U.S. General Accounting Office, *Terrorist Financing: U.S. Agencies Should Systematically Assess Terrorists' Use of Alternative Financing Mechanisms*, GAO-04-163 (Washington, D.C.: November 2003).

Two proposed legal initiatives are intended to enhance law enforcement efforts to thwart the smuggling of cigarettes into the United States. We did not evaluate the merits of these initiatives. A proposed bill called the Prevent All Cigarette Trafficking (PACT) Act would, among other things, lower the threshold for violating the Contraband Cigarette Trafficking Act (CCTA), a felony violation, from 60,000 to 10,000 cigarettes, increase ATF's authority to enter premises to enforce federal cigarette laws, and provide ATF the authority to use money generated during undercover sting operations to offset investigative expenses. Justice generally supports these provisions because they would enhance the tools to thwart cigarette smuggling. In addition, as part of the World Health Organization's (WHO) objective to address the rise and spread of tobacco consumption around the world, the Framework Convention on Tobacco Control (FCTC), a proposed international treaty, includes provisions that seek to eliminate the illicit trade in tobacco products, including cigarette smuggling. Among other provisions, the convention states that global cooperative action, including the exchange of cigarette tax information among countries, is an essential component in the effort to eliminate the illicit tobacco trade.

DHS and Justice reviewed a draft of this report and had no comments on the substance of the draft. Technical comments were incorporated as appropriate.

Background

Federal and State Excise Taxes Are Levied on Cigarettes Intended for Sale in the United States

Tobacco grows in many countries, but the United States has been the major source of the product for hundreds of years. About 500 billion genuine cigarettes were produced in domestic factories in 2003, and cigarettes continue to dominate the manufactured tobacco products market. Cigarette manufacturing is concentrated in Georgia, Kentucky, North Carolina, and Virginia.

After manufacture, the general industry pattern is for manufacturers to deposit cigarettes in warehouses and pay the federal cigarette excise tax of 39 cents per pack of 20 cigarettes. Next, the cigarettes move to a wholesaler stamping agent. Stamping agents have authority from states to affix to cigarette packs evidence of the payment of the appropriate state tax.[3] Once the stamping agent receives the unstamped cigarettes, it usually does not redistribute them until the state tax stamp has been affixed. After this is done, the stamping agent usually sells the cigarettes to other wholesalers (nonstamping agents), distributors, and retailers. As of January 1, 2004, the state excise tax rates for a pack of 20 cigarettes ranged from 2.5 cents in Virginia to $2.05 in New Jersey.

Tobacco products are also exported tax-free (federal and state) from manufacturers or from export warehouses. An export warehouse is a bonded warehouse, which stores tobacco products for subsequent shipment to a foreign country, Puerto Rico, the Virgin Islands, and other possessions of the United States. Export warehouses are typically located at the international borders with Mexico and Canada, at international airports that have a considerable number of international flights, and at seaports.

Domestic Cigarette Production Has Declined, While Imported Cigarettes Have Increased in Recent Years

Over the past decade, domestic cigarette production has declined, while U.S. imports of cigarettes have grown significantly. Figure 1 shows U.S. domestic cigarette production and cigarette imports from 1994 through 2003. In 2003, for example, cigarette production decreased by 32 billion cigarettes (6 percent) from 2002, and totaled 500 billion cigarettes, down from 532 billion cigarettes in 2002. On the other hand, imported cigarettes rose 24 percent to 25.9 billion cigarettes when compared with 2002 at 20.9 billion cigarettes.

---

[3]According to a Federation of Tax Administrators official, as of April 2004, 47 states required that tax stamps be placed on cigarette packages as evidence that state cigarette taxes were paid. North Dakota, North Carolina, and South Carolina do not require tax stamps.

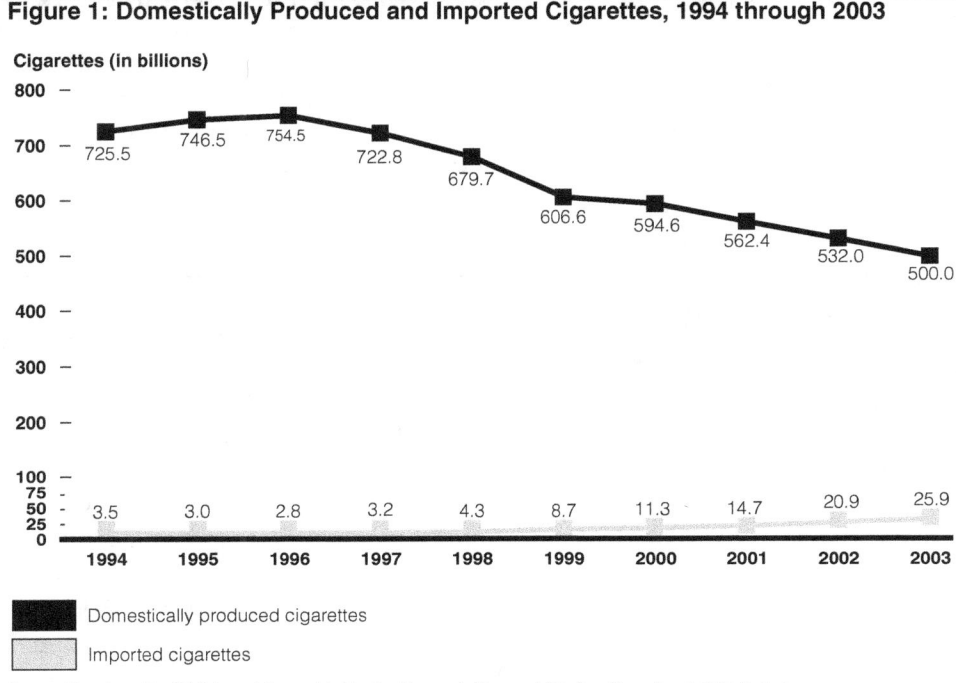

Figure 1: Domestically Produced and Imported Cigarettes, 1994 through 2003

Cigarettes (in billions)

	1994	1995	1996	1997	1998	1999	2000	2001	2002	2003
Domestically produced	725.5	746.5	754.5	722.8	679.7	606.6	594.6	562.4	532.0	500.0
Imported	3.5	3.0	2.8	3.2	4.3	8.7	11.3	14.7	20.9	25.9

■ Domestically produced cigarettes

☐ Imported cigarettes

Source: Developed by GAO from data provided by the Economic Research Service, Department of Agriculture.

Cigarettes Can be Diverted from the Distribution System

Cigarettes can be diverted from the normal distribution system in a number of ways, resulting in the evasion of cigarette taxes. According to an ATF report,[4] for example, "over-the-road" smuggling generally includes small purchases (well under 100 cartons; 10 packs per carton, 20 cigarettes per pack) in one state for transport to a higher-tax state for resale. Also, counterfeit stamping operations and manipulation of interstate cigarette distribution reports have been identified as potential major sources of revenue loss to the various states. These operations are characteristic of larger and more sophisticated criminal operations, possibly involving collusion between certain wholesalers and firms with outlets such as vending machines and retail stores.

[4]Department of the Treasury, Bureau of Alcohol, Tobacco and Firearms, *An Introduction to: the Bureau of Alcohol, Tobacco and Firearms and the Regulated Industries* (ATF P 5000.13, 12/98).

GAO-04-641 Cigarette Smuggling

Moreover, the illicit trade in smuggling both genuine and counterfeit cigarettes into the United States avoids both federal excise tax and state taxes on cigarettes. The major types of cigarette smuggling into the United States are: (1) smuggling of counterfeit cigarettes manufactured overseas and (2) smuggling of genuine cigarettes manufactured overseas but diverted to the illicit market. Untaxed, domestically produced cigarettes intended for export also can be diverted to the illicit market.

Cigarette Smuggling into the United States Considered a Significant Problem

While the extent of cigarette smuggling into the United States is unknown, ATF and ICE officials consider it a significant problem. Officials in these agencies note that cigarette smuggling activities attract international and domestic criminal groups with the lure of high profits and relatively low risk. The smuggling of cigarettes into the United States also results in lost federal and state excise tax revenue. However, the extent of the total lost tax revenue is unknown. Smuggled cigarettes, which include counterfeit and genuine brand cigarettes, also pose a public health risk as all cigarettes do; though, no studies have been done to determine whether counterfeit cigarettes pose a greater health risk than genuine brand cigarettes.

Intelligence Indicates Cigarette Smuggling Is a High Profit Crime with Possible Terrorism Connections

The smuggling of cigarettes into the United States is part of the worldwide illegal cigarette traffic, but the full extent of such smuggling is unknown. ATF and ICE do not have estimates of the quantity of cigarettes smuggled into the country, nor were we able to find any studies conducted by other organizations regarding the extent of the cigarette smuggling problem. There is evidence that both counterfeit and genuine brand cigarettes are smuggled into the United States and that criminals divert genuine cigarettes from legitimate distribution channels intended for sale outside the United States (e.g., foreign manufactured cigarettes held in U.S. warehouses awaiting trans-shipment to other countries and domestically manufactured cigarettes to be exported from the United States, including cigarettes for sale in duty free stores).

On the basis of cigarette investigations and intelligence collected, ATF and ICE officials said cigarette smuggling into the United States, particularly the smuggling of counterfeit cigarettes, is a significant problem. Indications are that the possibility of making huge profits has attracted criminals, including international and domestic organized crime groups, to smuggling. ATF and ICE officials noted that cigarette smuggling is also attractive to criminals because it is considered to be a relatively low risk crime, with penalties that are lower than the penalties for smuggling drugs.

According to an ATF report,[5] some cigarette smugglers have ties with terrorist groups, and there are indications that terrorist group involvement in illicit cigarette trafficking, as well as the relationship between criminal groups and terrorist groups, will grow in the future because of the large profits that can be made. In addition, according to ATF and ICE, organized crime groups sometimes launder proceeds of international cigarette smuggling through U.S. financial institutions.

ATF and ICE officials indicated that cigarettes are smuggled into the United States from many different countries. For example, according to ATF and ICE officials, smuggled cigarettes have been identified coming to the United States from China, Malaysia, Korea, Russia, Latvia, Mexico, Brazil, Paraguay, Uruguay, and the Philippines.

The ATF report also notes that cigarette trafficking had become big business by 1999. Many states, as well as many foreign countries, have increased cigarette taxes, resulting in a large difference in the wholesale price and the price paid by consumers at the retail level and creating potential illicit profits of $7 to $13 per carton of cigarettes. According to an ATF intelligence official, U.S. and European law enforcement information shows that illicit cigarette trafficking has become a multibillion dollar a year, worldwide crime phenomenon.

Cigarette Smuggling Results in Lost Revenues and Public Health Risk

Cigarette smuggling into the United States results in lost federal and state revenue. Each pack of cigarettes smuggled into the United States avoids the payment of $0.39 in federal cigarette excise tax, a median $0.0375 in customs import duties, and a median $0.60 in state excise tax.[6] The extent of these revenue losses, however, is unknown, because, as stated earlier, no one knows the extent of cigarette smuggling into the United States. Additionally, there are no reliable estimates of the overall amount of

---

[5]Bureau of Alcohol, Tobacco, Firearms and Explosives, *Illicit Cigarette Trafficking and the Funding of Terrorism*, July 22, 2003.

[6]According to ICE officials, states with higher cigarette excise taxes are generally the states that lose cigarette tax revenue due to smuggling. States could also lose other revenue. The Master Settlement Agreement, signed in November 1998 by the attorneys general of 46 states, the District of Columbia, and the 5 U.S. territories, requires four of the nation's largest tobacco companies to make annual payments to states as reimbursement for health care costs related to tobacco use. The annual payments are to be adjusted downward when a cigarette manufacturer's sales volume decreases, such as lost sales because consumers purchased smuggled cigarettes instead of legitimate cigarettes.

revenue that the federal and state governments are losing because of cigarettes being smuggled into the United States.

Furthermore, cigarettes, both counterfeit and genuine, pose a public health risk. There is no safe cigarette, the nation's largest cigarette manufacturers acknowledge. Since the release in 1964 of the first Surgeon General's report on smoking and health, scientific knowledge about the health consequences of tobacco use has greatly increased. As reported by the CDC, tobacco use, particularly smoking, remains the number one cause of preventable disease and death in the United States.

Officials at the CDC Office on Smoking and Health said that they have not done any studies and were not aware of any studies to determine whether counterfeit cigarettes posed additional risks. In addition, law enforcement and cigarette manufacturer laboratories that routinely analyze seized cigarettes do not test seized cigarettes for health risks.

Federal Agencies Increased Efforts to Thwart Cigarette Smuggling into the United States and Increased Seizures

ICE, ATF, and CBP are responsible for law enforcement activities to combat the smuggling of cigarettes into the United States, as part of their multifaceted missions. For example, through its Tobacco Program, ICE works to enforce U.S. laws related to tobacco smuggling for which it has investigative jurisdiction. ATF, which typically investigates smuggled cigarettes that have reached the domestic market, also enforces federal antitobacco smuggling laws, particularly the CCTA.[7] CBP inspectors operate at U.S. ports of entry, to detect illegal goods, including smuggled cigarettes, which might enter the country. CBP uses tools such as a targeting system and shipping manifest reviews to target incoming cargo for further examination. ICE and ATF officials said they have been conducting more cigarette smuggling investigations in recent years and described the agencies' current investigations as generally larger, more complex, and longer-term than previous investigations. Additionally, a CBP database shows that the number of cigarette seizures by CBP and ICE

---

[7]The CCTA (18 U.S.C. 2342) makes it unlawful (a felony) for any person to ship, transport, receive, possess, sell, distribute, or purchase more than 60,000 cigarettes that bear no evidence of state cigarette tax payment in the state in which the cigarettes are found, if such state requires a stamp or other indicia to be placed on cigarette packages to demonstrate payment of taxes. Certain persons, including permit holders under the Internal Revenue Code, common carriers with proper bills of lading, or individuals licensed by the state where the cigarettes are found, may possess these cigarettes. (See also 18 U.S.C. 2341.)

have increased dramatically, from 12 total seizures in 1998 to 191 seizures in 2003.

Several Federal Agency Missions Address Cigarette Smuggling

ICE, ATF, and CBP are involved in the fight against the illicit tobacco trade. Each agency addresses some aspect of cigarette smuggling as part of its multifaceted mission.

ICE Efforts to Combat Cigarette Smuggling

ICE has responsibility for the enforcement of immigration and customs laws within the United States. ICE investigates a range of offenses, including money laundering, smuggling—including cigarette smuggling— and fraud—including intellectual property rights (IPR) violations.[8] To carry out its responsibilities, ICE collects, analyzes, investigates, and disseminates intelligence data for use by enforcement operations.

ICE operational and tactical control of investigative and intelligence operations are divided geographically in the United States by areas of responsibility and managed by special agents-in-charge. The special agents-in-charge are responsible for the administration and management of all investigative customs enforcement activities within the geographic boundaries of the office. ICE also has special agents in 34 offices in 23 countries outside the United States—the special agents work with their foreign counterparts to help combat various crimes, including cigarette smuggling.

As part of its responsibilities, ICE's National Intellectual Property Rights Coordination Center (IPR Center), an interagency effort to coordinate a unified federal response regarding IPR violations (i.e., counterfeit goods), handled counterfeit tobacco product violations when it was started in February 2000.[9] In January 2001, responsibility for these violations was delegated from the IPR Center to a newly formed Tobacco Task Force.[10]

---

[8]IPR violations include trademark, trade name, and copyright violations, such as when cigarettes are clandestinely manufactured and given the label of a genuine brand name.

[9]The IPR Center was created before the U.S. Customs Service was transferred to DHS in March 2003.

[10]Starting in November 2003, the IPR Center was again given responsibility for addressing counterfeit cigarette violations. According to ICE officials, the Center coordinates its activities regarding counterfeit cigarettes with ICE's Tobacco Program.

According to ICE officials, the former U.S. Customs Service gave additional priority to efforts to combat a growing threat—cigarette smuggling—when it created the Tobacco Task Force. The task force was responsible for addressing the smuggling of both counterfeit and genuine cigarettes. The task force was created by the U.S. Customs Service in January 2001 with internal funds and was subsequently funded by an $800,000 congressional appropriation in fiscal year 2002. In fiscal year 2003, although there were no appropriations earmarked for the task force, ICE decided to maintain a focus on cigarette smuggling and changed the name to the Tobacco Program, according to the Tobacco Program Manager.

ICE officials said that ICE's Tobacco Program promotes and assists investigations and interdictions of tobacco smuggling, while not directly managing investigations. The program monitors, coordinates, and provides guidance to ICE, CBP, U.S. Attorneys' Offices, and foreign, state, and local law enforcement agencies on international smuggling matters. The program also provides training and reference material to investigators and works with ICE, CBP, ATF, and Treasury's Alcohol and Tobacco Tax and Trade Bureau (TTB) to address legal and policy issues related to tobacco smuggling. The program is staffed with two special agents and one intelligence analyst at ICE headquarters in Washington, D.C.

ATF Investigative Efforts

ATF is a law enforcement agency within the Department of Justice, responsible for enforcing federal laws and regulations relating to alcohol, tobacco, firearms, explosives, and arson. Regarding cigarettes, ATF seeks to reduce illegal cigarette trafficking in particular by enforcing the CCTA,[11] divest criminal and terrorist organizations of money derived from this illicit activity, and significantly reduce tax revenue losses to the states. ATF has offices located throughout the United States to conduct these investigations and has an array of employees that range from criminal investigators to inspectors, auditors, chemists, and other professionals.

ATF's tobacco diversion mission is to disrupt and eliminate criminal and terrorist organizations by identifying, investigating, and arresting offenders who traffic in contraband cigarettes; conduct financial investigations in

---

[11]Justice noted that on September 10, 2003, the Attorney General delegated to the Director of ATF authority to investigate violations under the Jenkins Act. The Jenkins Act (15 U.S.C. 375-378) requires any person who sells and ships cigarettes across a state line to a buyer, other than a licensed distributor, to report the sale to the buyer's state tobacco tax administrator.

GAO-04-641 Cigarette Smuggling

conjunction with tobacco diversion investigations in order to seize and deny further access to assets used by criminal enterprises and terrorist organizations; prevent criminal encroachment of the legitimate tobacco industry by organizations trafficking in cigarettes; and assist local, state, and other federal agencies with cigarette trafficking investigations.

ATF officials said the agency typically gets involved in cigarette smuggling investigations after the smuggled cigarettes enter the domestic market. The officials said that ATF investigators attempt to determine the source of the smuggled cigarettes; however, ATF does not often pursue investigations internationally.[12] The officials also noted that ATF coordinates its investigative efforts with ICE and other federal, state, and local agencies on a case-by-case basis.

ATF officials also told us that ATF's intelligence branch increased its emphasis on cigarette smuggling in 2000. According to the officials, ATF follows a two-pronged approach to tobacco intelligence: (1) strategic intelligence, which entails collecting intelligence from a variety of sources (such as ATF field offices, other law enforcement agencies, and the tobacco industry concerning counterfeit cigarettes), looking at cigarette trafficking patterns and trends and international terrorism links, and providing the developed intelligence to ATF field investigators and others; and (2) tactical intelligence, whereby analysts conduct analytical work to support about 20 to 25 investigations at a time.

CBP Inspection Efforts

CBP's priority mission is to prevent terrorists and terrorist weapons from entering the United States. Other CBP's mission responsibilities include: stemming the flow of illegal drugs and other contraband; protecting American businesses from theft of their intellectual property; regulating and facilitating international trade; collecting import duties; and enforcing U.S. trade laws. Thus, combating smuggling of both genuine and counterfeit cigarettes falls squarely within CBP's mission responsibilities. CBP officials explained that since September 11, 2001, overall CBP mission priorities for identifying and detecting illegal and harmful commodities coming into the country have shifted from narcotics smuggling to antiterrorism concerns. The priorities currently are

- #1 – antiterrorism;

---

[12]ATF could not break out its computerized investigation data to identify the number of investigations that were pursued outside the United States.

- #2 – narcotics smuggling; and

- #3 – trade commodities violations; textiles, toys, watches, and other items, including counterfeit and genuine smuggled cigarettes.

To perform its inspection duties, CBP has inspectors at ports of entry into the United States. In addition to staff at CBP's headquarters, officials at 20 field operations locations and at more than 300 ports of entry oversee the entry of all goods entering the United States. CBP also has 5 specific units, called Strategic Trade Centers, 2 of which analyze cigarette smuggling and provide information to other CBP units to assist in combating the problem.

We previously reported[13] that CBP's Commissioner said the large volume of imports and its limited resources make it impossible to physically inspect all oceangoing containers without disrupting the flow of commerce. The Commissioner also said it is unrealistic to expect that all containers warrant such inspection because each container poses a different level of risk based on a number of factors, including the exporter, the transportation providers, and the importer. To direct its resources toward higher-risk cargo and to minimize its impact on the flow of commerce, CBP has developed a layered approach to inspections. This approach includes: a targeting system, to assess the risk level of individual containers and to flag high-risk containers for physical inspection; a random inspection program; and the selection of containers for physical inspection based on a review of the shipping manifests and knowledge or intelligence gathered at the local ports. While most of the inspectors assigned to seaports perform physical inspections of goods entering the country, some are "targeters" – they review documents and intelligence reports and determine which cargo containers should undergo additional documentary reviews and/or physical inspections.

As part of its layered approach, CBP employs its Automated Targeting System (ATS) computer model to review documentation on all arriving containers to help select or "target" containers for additional documentary review and/or physical inspection, such as containers that may contain cigarettes being smuggled. The ATS was originally designed to help identify illegal narcotics in cargo containers. ATS automatically matches

---

[13]U.S. General Accounting Office, *Homeland Security: Preliminary Observations on Efforts to Target Security Inspections of Cargo Containers*, GAO-04-325T (Washington, D.C.: December 2003).

its targeting rules against the manifest and other available data for every arriving container and assigns a level of risk (i.e., low, medium, high) to each container. At the port level, inspectors use ATS, as well as other data (e.g., intelligence reports), to determine whether to inspect a particular container.

In addition, CBP has a program, called the Supply Chain Stratified Examination, which supplements ATS by randomly selecting additional containers to be physically examined. The results of the random inspection program are to be compared with the results of ATS inspections to improve targeting. If CBP officials decide to inspect a particular container, they might first use equipment such as the Vehicle and Cargo Inspection System that takes a gamma-ray image of the container so inspectors can see any visual anomalies. With or without this imaging system, inspectors can open a container and physically examine its contents.

At the Los Angeles/Long Beach seaport, we interviewed inspectors assigned to a unit called the Manifest Review Unit (MRU) that analyzes manifests, which list in detail the total cargo of vessels. Manifests are issued by carriers or their agents for specific voyages. Examples of data elements on a manifest include shipper, consignee, point and country of origin of goods, export carrier, port of lading, port of discharge, description of packages and goods, and date of lading.

CBP regulations require that manifest data be sent electronically to CBP 24 hours before cargo is loaded on a ship at a foreign port for shipment to the United States. CBP then determines whether the merchandise merits examination or immediate release. MRU is to review all manifested cargo for risk, based on ATS's rules and criteria, such as shipment from a country known to be a source of counterfeit cigarettes. MRU inspectors may also make additional computer queries based on their experience and/or specific intelligence about a shipper or commodity.

After MRU selects cargo for examination, it is sent to a Centralized Examination Station, which is a privately operated facility at which imported merchandise identified for physical examination is unloaded and made available to CBP examination team inspectors. If an examination results in a finding of smuggled cigarettes, a sample is taken to determine whether they are counterfeit or genuine, the merchandise is seized and forfeited, counterfeit cigarettes are destroyed, and genuine cigarettes may be destroyed or auctioned. After the examination is complete, the inspectors notify MRU of the results of the examination. MRU inspectors may then use the information for future targeting of cargo for examination.[14]

CBP officials said that although cigarettes are not necessarily being targeted as a specific imported commodity to be physically inspected at a port, targeting rules or criteria are constantly being updated from tips received from many different sources, and consequently many illegally imported goods, including cigarettes, are discovered through the targeting process.

Figures 2, 3, and 4 show a likeness of the container in which recently seized counterfeit cigarettes were shipped, how they were packaged as legitimate merchandise, and what they looked like when unloaded and inspected.

---

[14]According to ICE officials, an ICE investigation may also be initiated in this process. In addition, the officials said active ICE investigations develop information that results in seizures by CBP or ICE.

Figure 2: A Typical 40-foot Shipping Container at the Los Angeles/Long Beach Examination Station

Source: CBP.

Figure 3: Smuggled Counterfeit Cigarettes Disguised as Legitimate Merchandise

Source: CBP.

Note: After unloading the container, two different types of shipping boxes were discovered that were labeled as the same type of legitimate merchandise. The boxes on the left contained the merchandise, while the boxes on the right contained counterfeit cigarettes.

Figure 4: Smuggled Counterfeit Cigarettes

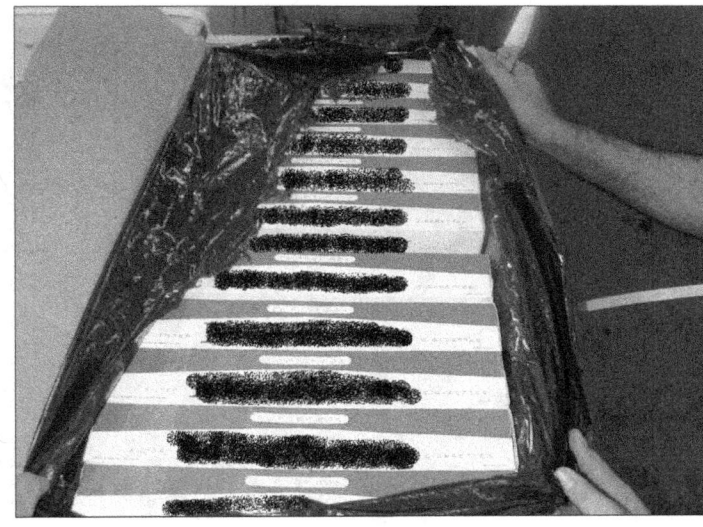

Source: CBP.

Number of ICE and ATF Investigations into Cigarette Smuggling Have Increased and Become Larger and More Complex

ICE and ATF are responsible for investigating cigarette smuggling. Both agencies initiate and carry out their own investigations and sometimes work together in conducting joint investigations. ICE investigates organized international cigarette smuggling, including illegal activities related to the smuggling of cigarettes into the United States. ATF's cigarette smuggling investigations usually involve interstate smuggling activities. When ATF determines that the smuggled cigarettes originated outside the United States, the investigation may broaden to pursue criminal activities related to international cigarette smuggling.

According to the Tobacco Program Manager, ICE cigarette smuggling investigations have increased and become more complex and longer term since 2001. ICE officials told us that the Tobacco Program has focused on encouraging the development of larger investigations to identify and dismantle entire organizations responsible for cigarette smuggling, including investigating the potential for ties to terrorist groups.[15]

---

[15] According to ICE officials, as of May 2004, ICE was not aware of any indictments that connected material support of terrorism to the smuggling of cigarettes into or out of the United States.

Figure 5 shows the number of ICE cigarette-related investigations initiated and closed for each fiscal year from 1998 through 2003.[16]

Figure 5: Number of ICE Cigarette-Related Investigations Initiated and Closed, Fiscal Years 1998 through 2003

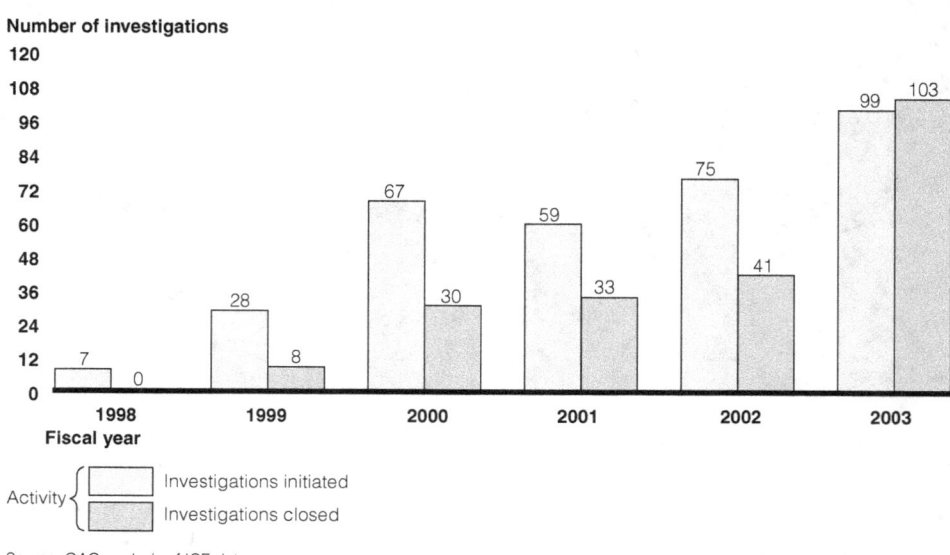

Source: GAO analysis of ICE data.

One large, complex ICE investigation, for example, (supported by CBP, ATF, and other agencies) began in the fall of 2000 and concluded in January 2004 and was characterized as the largest probe to date involving the smuggling of cigarettes into the United States. The investigation resulted in a 92-count federal indictment against defendants accused of participating in a scheme to smuggle into the nation more than 107 million genuine and counterfeit cigarettes with a potential street value of $37.5 million.

---

[16]Cigarette-related investigations include the smuggling of counterfeit or genuine cigarettes into the United States, smuggling cigarettes into foreign countries, smuggling cigarettes in violation of embargoes, and international money laundering when one of the underlying crimes is tobacco-related (e.g., cigarette smuggling, trafficking in counterfeit cigarettes, trafficking in stolen cigarettes, and interstate smuggling to avoid state cigarette taxes).

GAO-04-641 Cigarette Smuggling

We also visited with an ICE supervisory special agent in Long Beach, who noted there has been a huge increase in counterfeit cigarettes seized since early 2002, although it is hard to tell if the volume of smuggling has increased or more is being detected because of the tightening of security since September 11, 2001. The supervisory special agent said that cigarette smuggling investigations have become complex and time-consuming, as ICE is taking a long-term approach to cigarette smuggling investigations. ICE wants to study and understand the whole cycle of smuggling operations so that it can dismantle key organizations responsible for cigarette smuggling.

ATF also reported an increase in recent years in the number of tobacco investigations. According to ATF officials, nationwide, ATF had about 260 cigarette smuggling investigations ongoing in August 2003. The 260 investigations primarily involved the smuggling of cigarettes from state-to-state rather than into the United States. Figure 6 shows the number of ATF tobacco investigations initiated and closed for each fiscal year from 1998 through 2003.[17]

---

[17]ATF tobacco investigations primarily involve cigarettes. Some investigations involve the smuggling of counterfeit or genuine cigarettes into the United States, and some involve only domestic, interstate cigarette smuggling. ATF could not break out its computerized investigation data to identify the number of investigations that involved cigarette smuggling into the United States and to identify those that involved counterfeit and genuine cigarettes.

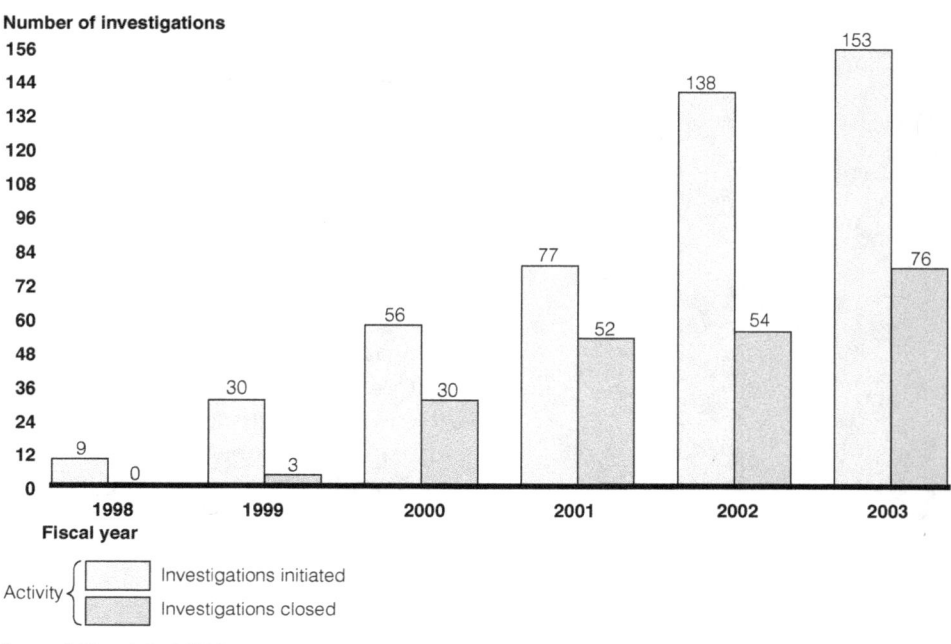

Source: GAO analysis of ATF data.

An ATF official told us that generally, cigarette investigations take 12 to 24 months, and the investigations are extensive and complex, particularly the more recent investigations which are still ongoing. The ATF official said that unlike in the past where ATF just seized the cigarettes and vehicles because the smuggling was being performed by "mom and pop" operations, since about 1999 more cigarette smuggling is being carried out by criminal organizations and, therefore, requires much more extensive investigation. In addition, ATF reported in August 2003 that it had identified 8 of its investigations initiated in fiscal years 2002 and 2003 as linked to terrorism. ATF officials noted that the majority of its counterfeit cigarette investigations involve cigarettes smuggled into the United States.

Cigarette Seizures Have Increased

In addition to the rise in cigarette smuggling investigations by ICE and ATF, the number of illegal cigarettes seized by CBP and ICE has increased. While the number of seizures (with an estimated value of $2,500 or greater) of genuine cigarettes exceeded counterfeit cigarette seizures, the quantity and estimated value of counterfeit cigarettes seized exceeded genuine cigarettes.[18] For example, in fiscal year 2003, CBP and ICE made 56 seizures of counterfeit cigarettes, with an estimated value of $45.8 million, and 135 seizures of genuine cigarettes, with an estimated value of $5.1 million. Table 1 shows the number and estimated value of counterfeit and genuine cigarettes seized by CBP and ICE in each fiscal year from 1998 through 2003.

Table 1: Seizures of Counterfeit and Genuine Cigarettes, Fiscal Years 1998 through 2003

Cigarettes	1998		1999		2000		2001		2002		2003	
Number of seizures	0	12	3	29	11	39	10	56	34	163	56	135
Estimated value	0	$1,383,650	$348,705	$1,136,338	$4,242,232	$1,333,768	$5,787,872	$7,708,890	$34,483,613	$7,924,351	$45,817,162	$5,075,053
Estimated number of cartons	0	79,277	19,926	65,794	354,606	96,843	272,939	322,351	1,286,045	554,670	1,797,431	225,981

☐ Counterfeit cigarettes
▨ Genuine cigarettes

Source: Developed by GAO from CBP's database.

Note: Data include only seizures that have an estimated value of $2,500 or greater to exclude seizures of cigarettes transported by individuals and intended for personal consumption.

Most counterfeit cigarette seizures were at the Los Angeles/Long Beach seaport.[19] CBP officials at the Los Angeles/Long Beach seaport said that they began to see more counterfeit cigarettes being seized near the end of 2001. Specifically, 3 of 10 (30 percent) counterfeit cigarette seizures nationwide were made at the Los Angeles/Long Beach seaport in fiscal year 2001; these increased to 21 of 34 (62 percent) in fiscal year 2002 and to 26 of 56 (46 percent) in fiscal year 2003. The officials said that they believe the increase in seizures of counterfeit cigarettes was due to better intelligence and better inspections – based on electronic methods such as

---

[18]CBP and ICE seize genuine cigarettes that are diverted from legitimate distribution channels and are being smuggled into the United States to avoid the payment of taxes.

[19]The Los Angeles/Long Beach seaport is the busiest port in the United States, with over 2.8 million 40-foot containers in-bound per year. Forty-three percent of containers coming in to the United States passes through the Los Angeles/Long Beach seaport; approximately 9,000 per day.

ATS targeting of cargo for inspection and the ICE Tobacco Program, which has helped to bring the problem of cigarette smuggling to the forefront and has, therefore, led to more seizures.

CBP data also showed a rise in the value of counterfeit cigarette seizures compared to other commodities. Figure 7 shows the percent of counterfeit cigarettes increasing from 9 percent of commodities seized in fiscal year 2000 to 44 percent in fiscal year 2003.

Figure 7: Top Counterfeit Seizures by Commodity, Fiscal Years 2000 through 2003

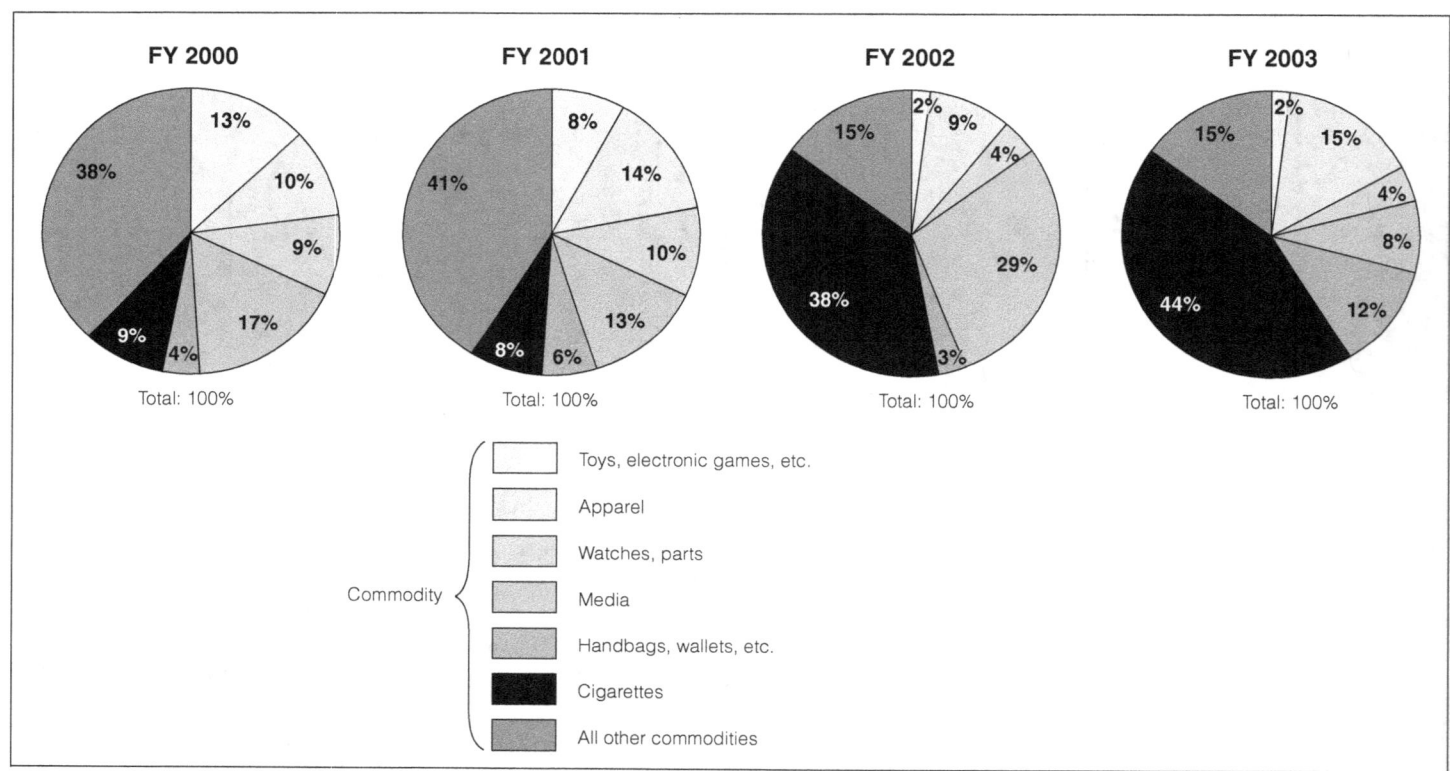

Source: Developed by GAO from CBP data.

Legal Initiatives Being Pursued to Help Thwart Cigarette Smuggling

Two legal initiatives have been proposed to enhance efforts to thwart the cigarette smuggling problem. We did not evaluate the merits of these initiatives. However, the Department of Justice generally supports certain provisions contained in the PACT Act,[20] a bill intended to combat cigarette smuggling, but has not formally endorsed the Act. In addition, WHO has proposed an international treaty, the FCTC, to enhance global actions directed against the illicit tobacco trade, including cigarette smuggling.

Justice Suggested Three Legal Initiatives to Combat Cigarette Smuggling

In October 2003, Justice suggested that Congress could strengthen the enforcement tools for combating cigarette smuggling by: (1) lowering the threshold for violating CCTA[21] (a felony violation) from 60,000 to 30,000 cigarettes, (2) giving ATF authority to use money generated during undercover sting operations to offset investigative expenses, and (3) increasing ATF's authority to enter premises to enforce federal cigarette laws.

The PACT Act, a bill intended to combat cigarette smuggling, includes some of Justice's suggestions. However, Justice has not formally endorsed the PACT Act (or its House companion bill, H.R. 2824). If enacted, the PACT Act would broaden the definition of what constitutes contraband cigarettes by lowering the CCTA quantity for nontaxed cigarettes to be considered contraband from 60,000 to 10,000. This is a lower threshold than Justice suggested. But, according to the bill's sponsors, lowering the contraband cigarette threshold would allow ATF to open more investigations and seek more federal felony prosecutions of cigarette smugglers.

Second, the bill would allow ATF to pay expenses of undercover investigations with money accrued during such operations. Justice supports this provision. For example, as part of an undercover investigation, ATF could sell cigarettes to a suspect and use the cash to pay informants or buy more cigarettes from traffickers in the investigation. This would make ATF's powers more comparable to those of other investigative agencies like the Federal Bureau of Investigation and the Drug Enforcement Administration, which may use such nonappropriated

---

[20]The proposed PACT Act (S. 1177), a bill introduced on June 3, 2003, by Senators Orrin G. Hatch and Herb Kohl, contains provisions intended to, among other things, prevent tobacco smuggling and ensure the collection of all tobacco taxes.

[21]P.L. 95-575, Nov. 2, 1978.

funds to make undercover purchases and pay other investigative expenses.

Finally, the bill includes a provision that would authorize ATF to enter the property of any person who delivered, shipped, sold, distributed, or received more than 10,000 cigarettes a month to inspect cigarettes on the premises and any legal records or information on the cigarettes required by law. Justice supports increasing ATF's authority to enter premises to enforce federal cigarette laws, but it has not opined its views on whether the 10,000 cigarette threshold is appropriate. Currently, ATF must obtain consent to enter a person's property and conduct an inspection. If denied entry, ATF must obtain a search warrant by demonstrating probable cause to a U.S. district court judge to enter a person's property. Under the bill, if ATF is denied entry, its right of inspection could be enforced by a district court order with the submission of an affidavit or other evidence that entry was denied. As of April 2004, the PACT Act had passed the Senate and was referred to the House, where action was pending.

International Initiative Calls for Global Cooperative Action to Reduce the Illicit Tobacco Trade

FCTC seeks to address the rise and spread of tobacco consumption around the world through global solutions to a problem that cuts across national boundaries, cultures, societies and socioeconomic strata. FCTC, if ratified, would be an additional legal instrument addressing issues as diverse as tobacco advertising and promotion, agricultural diversification, smuggling, taxes, and subsidies.

FCTC was adopted at the World Health Assembly on May 21, 2003, and is open to all members of the WHO or the United Nations from June 2003 to June 2004 for ratification. At least 40 countries must ratify FCTC for it to become law. If FCTC is ratified, those ratifying nations would develop protocols, which are separate agreements containing specific measures designed to implement the broad goals called for by the FCTC. As of April 2004, the United States had not ratified FCTC.[22] The State Department, with interagency and White House input, was reviewing FCTC, including determining whether joining the convention would require any new legislation. According to the Director of Health Programs, State Department, that deliberative review process was moving forward. There is no set time frame for the review process to be completed.

---

[22]As of April 16, 2004, 10 countries had ratified FCTC.

As part of its objective, FCTC states that cooperative action is necessary to eliminate all forms of illicit trade in cigarettes and other tobacco products, including smuggling, illicit manufacturing and counterfeiting. Article 15 of FCTC (see app. II) is the only one of 38 Articles that addresses the illicit trade in tobacco products, including cigarette smuggling.

The first of seven measures in Article 15 states that the elimination of all forms of illicit trade in tobacco products, including smuggling, illicit manufacturing and counterfeiting, and the development and implementation of related national law, in addition to subregional, regional and global agreements, are essential components of tobacco control. The other measures require each ratifying country to, among other things, mark packages of tobacco products to control their movement, cooperate in investigations and prosecutions, periodically report progress made, and adopt other measures as appropriate to prevent illicit trade.

The fourth measure requires actions aimed at eliminating illicit trade in tobacco products. For example, one action that FCTC will require is the exchange of tax information among governments, as appropriate, and in accordance with national law and relevant applicable bilateral or multilateral agreements. Under present law, Section 6103 of the Internal Revenue Code (IRC) of 1986 in general provides that the government shall not disclose any taxpayer returns or return information. Section 6103(k)(4) of the IRC, however, permits the government to disclose such information ". . . to a competent authority of a foreign government which has an income tax or gift and estate tax convention, or other convention or bilateral agreement relating to the exchange of tax information, with the United States but only to the extent provided in, and subject to the terms and conditions of, such convention or bilateral agreement." According to the Assistant Chief Counsel of the Treasury Department's Alcohol and Tobacco Tax and Trade Bureau (TTB), FCTC is a convention that under Section 6103(k)(4) would allow the government, under the appropriate circumstances, to share taxpayer returns or return information with competent authorities of foreign governments who are Parties to FCTC.

According to TTB, the sharing of cigarette tax information with other countries could help government agencies determine when cigarette exports are diverted from legitimate distribution channels. Presently, when a U.S. company exports cigarettes to another country, the exporter files a document with TTB disclosing the type and quantity of cigarettes being exported with no federal cigarette excise taxes due or paid—this is considered taxpayer information. Currently, IRC does not allow TTB to provide this information to the country to which the cigarettes are shipped. The convention would allow the information to be provided and used to determine whether the quantity of cigarettes declared as imports matches the quantity of cigarettes exported. If the imported quantity is less than the exported quantity, this may indicate that some of the cigarettes were diverted to be smuggled into that or some other country, or back to the United States, without the payment of cigarette taxes and import duties.

Agency Comments

We provided a draft copy of this report to DHS and Justice. DHS and Justice had no comments on the substance of our draft. However, DHS and Justice provided technical comments which we have incorporated, as appropriate.

As agreed, unless you publicly announce the contents of this report earlier, we plan no further distribution of it until 30 days from the date of this letter. We will then send copies to others who are interested and make copies available to others who request them. In addition, the report will be available at no charge on GAO's Web site at http://www.gao.gov.

If you or your staffs have any questions regarding this report, please contact Darryl W. Dutton at (213) 830-1086 or me at (202) 512-8777. Key contributors to this report are listed in appendix III.

Paul L. Jones, Director
Homeland Security and Justice Issues

Appendix I: Scope and Methodology

To determine what is known about the nature and scope of the problem of smuggled cigarettes, including counterfeit cigarettes, entering the United States, we obtained information from the Department of Homeland Security's (DHS) U.S. Immigration and Customs Enforcement (ICE) and the Department of Justice's Bureau of Alcohol, Tobacco, Firearms and Explosives (ATF). We interviewed ICE and ATF headquarters officials in Washington, D.C., and we collected and reviewed pertinent documentation, such as an ATF report on cigarette trafficking and terrorism issued in July 2003.

We also contacted officials of various organizations to obtain information about the consequences of cigarette smuggling. To determine federal and state tax revenue losses due to the smuggling of cigarettes, including counterfeit cigarettes, into the United States, we interviewed headquarters officials in Washington, D.C., representing ICE, ATF, and the Department of the Treasury's Alcohol and Tobacco Tax and Trade Bureau (TTB); collected and reviewed available ATF documentation; and conducted an Internet search using a major Internet search engine (Google). To determine potential health risks due to the smuggling of cigarettes, including counterfeit cigarettes, into the United States, we interviewed officials representing TTB, DHS's U.S. Customs and Border Protection (CBP), the Centers for Disease Control and Prevention (CDC), and three tobacco manufacturers (Philip Morris U.S.A., Brown and Williamson Tobacco Corporation, and R. J. Reynolds Tobacco Company), and we collected information from CDC.

To determine federal law enforcement agencies' efforts to thwart the smuggling of cigarettes into the United States, we interviewed ICE, ATF, and CBP headquarters officials in Washington, D.C., and we collected and reviewed pertinent documentation, including data on the number of ICE cigarette-related investigations and ATF tobacco investigations initiated and closed and CBP and ICE cigarette seizures for selected fiscal years. We also interviewed an ICE official at a field office in Long Beach, California, ATF officials at the Los Angeles Field Division, and CBP officials at the Los Angeles/Long Beach seaport, which was identified as having the largest number of cigarette seizures in the country.

To assess the reliability of the ICE and ATF investigation data, we (1) reviewed existing information about the data and systems that produced them and (2) interviewed agency officials knowledgeable about the data as necessary. For the CBP and ICE seizure data, which CBP maintains in a database, CBP officials updated and provided us with data on the more significant cigarette seizures with estimated values of

$2,500 or greater. We focused on these seizures because CBP reported that smaller cigarette seizures are more likely to be instances of individuals transporting cigarettes intended for personal consumption rather than organized smuggling. To assess the reliability of the CBP and ICE seizure data, we (1) performed electronic testing for obvious errors in accuracy and completeness, (2) reviewed existing information about the data and systems that produced them, and (3) interviewed agency officials knowledgeable about the data. We determined that the investigation and seizure data were sufficiently reliable for this report.

To obtain information on certain legal initiatives being pursued to enhance law enforcement efforts to thwart the smuggling of cigarettes into the United States, we obtained information from the Justice Department in Washington, D.C., regarding the Prevent All Trafficking Act (S. 1177), a bill introduced in Congress with action pending at the time of our review, and we interviewed an ATF headquarters official. We also interviewed headquarters officials at the Department of State and TTB in Washington, D.C., and obtained information from the World Health Organization Web site regarding the Framework Convention on Tobacco Control, a proposed treaty initiated by the World Health Assembly.

For the background section, we obtained data on the number of cigarettes manufactured in the United States and the number of imported cigarettes from the Economic Research Service, U.S. Department of Agriculture, Web site; state cigarette excise tax rates from the Federation of Tax Administrators' Web site; the number of states using tax stamps as evidence that state cigarette taxes were paid from a Federation of Tax Administrators official; and the federal cigarette excise tax rate from ICE. The data were used for background purposes and were not verified.

We conducted our work between August 2003 and March 2004 in accordance with generally accepted government auditing standards.

Appendix II: Article 15 of the World Health Organization Framework Convention on Tobacco Control

Article 15: Illicit Trade in Tobacco Products

1. The Parties recognize that the elimination of all forms of illicit trade in tobacco products, including smuggling, illicit manufacturing and counterfeiting, and the development and implementation of related national law, in addition to subregional, regional and global agreements, are essential components of tobacco control.

2. Each Party shall adopt and implement effective legislative, executive, administrative or other measures to ensure that all unit packets and packages of tobacco products and any outside packaging of such products are marked to assist Parties in determining the origin of tobacco products, and in accordance with national law and relevant bilateral or multilateral agreements, assist Parties in determining the point of diversion and monitor, document and control the movement of tobacco products and their legal status. In addition, each Party shall:

    (a) require that unit packets and packages of tobacco products for retail and wholesale use that are sold on its domestic market carry the statement: "Sales only allowed jn (insert name of the country, subnational, regional or federal unit)" or carry any other effective marking indicating the final destination or which would assist authorities in determining whether the product is legally for sale on the domestic market; and

    (b) consider, as appropriate, developing a practical tracking and tracing regime that would further secure the distribution system and assist in the investigation of illicit trade.

3. Each Party shall require that the packaging information or marking specified in paragraph 2 of this Article shall be presented in legible form and/or appear in its principal language or languages.

4. With a view to eliminating illicit trade in tobacco products, each Party shall:

    (a) monitor and collect data on cross-border trade in tobacco products, including illicit trade, and exchange information among customs, tax and other authorities, as appropriate, and in accordance with national law and relevant applicable bilateral or multilateral agreements;

    (b) enact or strengthen legislation, with appropriate penalties and remedies, against illicit trade in tobacco products, including counterfeit and contraband cigarettes;

    (c) take appropriate steps to ensure that all confiscated manufacturing equipment, counterfeit and contraband cigarettes and other tobacco products are destroyed, using environmentally-friendly methods where feasible, or disposed of in accordance with national law;

GAO-04-641 Cigarette Smuggling

(d) adopt and implement measures to monitor, document and control the storage and distribution of tobacco products held or moving under suspension of taxes or duties within its jurisdiction; and

(e) adopt measures as appropriate to enable the confiscation of proceeds derived from the illicit trade in tobacco products.

5. Information collected pursuant to subparagraphs 4(a) and 4(d) of this Article shall, as appropriate, be provided in aggregate form by the Parties in their periodic reports to the Conference of the Parties, in accordance with Article 21.

6. The Parties shall, as appropriate and in accordance with national law, promote cooperation between national agencies, as well as relevant regional and international intergovernmental organizations as it relates to investigations, prosecutions and proceedings, with a view to eliminating illicit trade in tobacco products. Special emphasis shall be placed on cooperation at regional and subregional levels to combat illicit trade of tobacco products.

7. Each Party shall endeavour to adopt and implement further measures including licensing, where appropriate, to control or regulate the production and distribution of tobacco products in order to prevent illicit trade.

Appendix III: GAO Contacts and Staff Acknowledgments

GAO Contacts	Paul L. Jones (202) 512-8777 Darryl W. Dutton (213) 830-1086
Staff Acknowledgments	In addition to the above, Ronald G. Viereck, Daniel R. Garcia, Brian J. Lipman, Kathryn G. Young, Michelle C. Fejfar, Charles W. Bausell Jr., and Shirley A. Jones made key contributions to this report.